ABOUT THE AUTHOR

Born and raised in inner city Birmingham, Alan Hammond has since lived and worked as a family lawyer in North Yorkshire and London. Having brought up their three sons, he and his wife Eileen now live near Ross-on-Wye where he devotes his retirement time to his hobby of many years – namely, writing poetry and fiction. His book, *All's Fair in Love and Law*, was published in 2011 and he has now been persuaded to put some of his poems into the public domain in the hope that others may share the humour, emotion and pleasure evoked by these verses.

DEDICATION

To my wife, Eileen, our three sons, three daughters-in-law and eight grandchildren, who make my life worth living.

Alan C. Hammond

WHEN BOTH ENDS MEET

and other poems

AUSTIN MACAULEY PUBLISHERS™

LONDON • CAMBRIDGE • NEW YORK • SHARJAH

A CIP catalogue record for this title is available from the British
Library.

ISBN 9781398423978 (Paperback)
ISBN 9781398423985 (ePub e-book)

www.austinmacauley.com

First Published (2021)
Austin Macauley Publishers Ltd
25 Canada Square
Canary Wharf
London
E14 5LQ

THE POWER OF POETRY

Breaking news: *"A man and his wife embarked upon a steep climb with the intention of gaining access to a water supply. In doing so, the man fell and sustained a serious injury and, whilst running to help him, his wife also fell."*

Will you remember that in years to come?
OK, try this:
"Jack and Jill went up the hill to fetch a pail of water.
Jack fell down and broke his crown and Jill came tumbling after."

How many years is it since you first heard that? And it's stayed with you. Why is that? Is it the fact that it rhymes (more or less}? Or perhaps it's the metre or rhythm of the words as you read them? Whatever the reason, it is a fact that something expressed in the form of a poem (whether a nursery rhyme or a Shakespearian sonnet) penetrates more deeply into our consciousness than is the case with mere prose.

The purpose of this collection of assorted poems is not to demonstrate my poetic skills (?), but to share with you various thoughts and ideas which occur to us all from time to time. Some of these items are serious, some humorous, some downright silly, but they all relate to aspects of this extraordinary and varied life on Earth which we all have in common.

I'll keep in touch with you as you read on – you'll find I've placed a little introductory comment before each poem. So if any of the items stir up any views of your own, then why not scribble them in?… Unless, of course, you've borrowed the book from someone else, in which case do hand it back in pristine condition!

ALAN C. HAMMOND

POEMS

Without darkness, we wouldn't recognise light. Likewise, without evil,
we wouldn't recognise good. What do you think?

WHEN BOTH ENDS MEET

'Twas a warm September evening, shortly before dark,
When Santa Claus and Lucifer were walking in the park.
As each espied the other, some embarrassment took place;
While neither knew the other's name, each recognized the face.

Santa Claus, off duty, was attired in shirt and slacks;
His beard was trimmed, his hair was neat – no sign of toys or sacks.
Lucifer wore Harris Tweed, his tie a fetching red.
A trilby hat completely hid the horns upon his head.

"Good Evening to you," Santa said, "a very pleasant day!"
"Indeed it is," said Lucifer, then wondered what to say.
A park bench stood near where they spoke, close by a rustic stile
And Santa, just to beak the ice, said "shall we sit a while?"

"By all means," Lucifer replied, "let's sit down over there,
An admirable spot in which to take the evening air."
And there they sat, companionably, 'midst flower beds and trees –
Two elderly, distinguished-looking gentlemen at ease.

"I must admit," said Santa Claus, "it's nice to rest one's feet -
"Particularly at this time of year – this awful heat!"
"Ah, now," replied the other man, "you see, if truth be told,
I've always been the opposite I can't abide the cold!"

"How dull 'twould be," said Santa Claus, "if we were all the same.
Variety, I do believe, prevents life getting tame!"
"How right you are; I've always thought that," Lucifer agreed.
"Why should we all conform to this or that – there's just no need."

Santa nodded, knowingly, "I said that just last week –
Every man and woman has the right to be unique."
"Exactly so," said Lucifer. "What line of work d'you do?"
"Charity" replied the other, "Love and Hope – and you?"

"I'm in the furnace trade, " he said, "the Fire and Brimstone King.
Eternal Anguish, Grief and Woe – you know the sort of thing."
"Sounds interesting," said Santa "though I'm sure I couldn't do it –
I don't think I could bear to see those sinners going through it."

"You learn to be professional," said Lucifer. "Detached.
It's just so many damaged souls that have to be dispatched.
But your job, now, that's different – I don't know how you cope.
The pressure of those kids expecting all that Love and Hope!"

The two men sat there, quietly, reflecting upon Life
In all its vast diversity, its harmony and strife.
Then as the shadows lengthened and a chill came to the air,
They each got up and stretched their legs, grown stiff from sitting there.

"Time to go" said Lucifer, "Fires don't light themselves."
"I'd best be off too," Santa said. "Must go and sort those Elves."
The pair shook hands and both agreed that parting was a shame.
Then each went back to business,,, and Life went on just the same.

OLIVER COURT

Oliver Court was remarkably short,
Or, to put it more kindly – 'petite'.
Four feet six inches dead from the top of his head
To the soles of his rather small feet.

His friends didn't mind – they were always most kind;
They pretended they just hadn't seen
His acute lack of height – they were much too polite,
But, when all's said and done, well... I mean!

Being so close to the ground, as he very soon found,
Reduced him to a physical wreck.
By trying to walk tall he had many a fall
And a permanent crick in his neck.

He was very aware that it just wasn't fair.
His nerves were beginning to suffer.
He sought the advice of a Doctor called Grice,
A distinguished and learned old buffer.

He went in and sat down. Doctor Grice wore a frown,
A tall man, not much over forty,
Who leaned back in his chair with a self-righteous air,
And said, "What can I do for you, Shorty?"

At this, Oliver cried – he still had his pride.
A medical man he'd consulted.
He'd made up his mind – but what does he find?
The minute he's there, he's insulted.

With a pattering of feet, he ran out in the street,
Crying, "No more! I'd be better off dead!"
He ran under a truck, but what terrible luck
The thing passed right over his head.

Determined to die, to a tower block high
He proceeded, and ran through the door,
He climbed on a ledge, forced himself to the edge,
And he jumped from the 20th floor!

But strange to relate, he did not meet his fate,
'Cos he fell through a hole in the ground.
'Twas a sewer, you see – flushed him out to the sea,
And there, our poor Oliver drowned.

St Peter was there, plucking souls from the air,
To the Angels he said, with a snigger,
"We shouldn't make jokes, but look at this folks -
We'll chuck this one back till it's bigger!"

*When I was younger (much younger!), I worked for a while in a large office,
where I was one of a great number of junior clerks. The work was not particularly
stimulating and time tended to drag. But, just occasionally...*

MISS HARGREAVES

Miss Hargreaves through the office walks
Past fourteen clerks with eyes on stalks.
Invoices and ledgers lie
Neglected as she passes by,
Her shorthand notebook gently pressed
Against her smartly tailored breast.

Between the desks her high heels tap,
As glasses mist and pencils snap.
Passing through, quite unaware
Of fourteen clerks with rumpled hair
And greatly increased respiration,
She goes upstairs to take dictation.

MR TOMLINSON

I had a little budgie once,
With feathers green and blue.
I called him Mr Tomlinson –
It seemed the thing to do.

He'd sit upon his little perch
And talk of this and that,
Of ships and shoes and sealing wax,
And next door's ginger cat.

He was a happy little bird,
I loved him quite a lot,
But he developed whooping cough,
And so I had him shot.

There are lots of things in nature that we don't understand
(including human beings!). Here's just one example...

THE GOOSEBERRY'S PLIGHT

Our pathway through life as we frequently find,
Is littered with worries and cares.
But the question which constantly nags at my mind
Is: "Why does a gooseberry have hairs?"

Philosophers ponder the meaning of life;
Churchmen debate who is right;
Our Statesmen seek glory through power and strife
But what of the gooseberry's plight ?

Charles Darwin informed us that all living things
Adapt to their natural state,
Which accounts for the fact that all sparrows have wings,
And the horns on the antelope's pate.

But somehow it seems things have gone badly wrong,
And this is what's worrying me:
The hairs on the gooseberry don't seem to belong.
What possible use can they be ?

"Very, good!" you may say, "most amusing – Ha! Ha!
We'll forgive Nature's little omission.
There are plenty of things more important by far,
Than the gooseberry's hirsute condition."

You're free to poke fun if you choose – free
To say I'm just making a fuss.
But if Nature slipped up with the gooseberry,
Might she not have done likewise...with us ?

PARSON CEDRIC ROSE

A most amazing tale is that of Parson Cedric Rose,
Who woke up one fine day to find he'd grown another nose.
The nose that he'd been born with was still firmly in its place,
But now there was a second, rather higher up his face.

He thought "that's most unusual, in fact it's rather odd.
It must be part of some great plan – a bounteous gift from God.
The Lord be praised! – a precious boon hath been bestowed on me!"
And then his housekeeper came in to bring his morning tea.

She said, "Good morning Vicar – Good Gracious! I declare!
You went to bed with one nose, and now you've got a pair!"
The parson rose and dressed himself, then hurried out in haste –
The Bishop he must now consult, there was no time to waste.

The Bishop's Chaplain greeted him – a most respectful man.
"Good Morning, Vicar" he intoned – "Forgive me, if you can,
But may I venture to point out that since you rose from slumber,
Your reverend features now exceed the customary number."

The Vicar waved the man aside – "I'm well aware of that.
It is in an honour from above – now kindly take my hat."

The Bishop was consuming toast and soft-boiled eggs and tea
When Parson Rose announced himself: "My Lord! as you can see
A miracle has happened – let us praise the Holy Ghost."
"Good God!" said my Lord Bishop, with his mouth quite full of toast.

"My Son, you have been blessed indeed of all the Human Race,
It is a sign from God on High ...Two noses on one face!"

The Reverend Cedric Rose was very shortly made a Saint.
The world's most famous artists his portrait they did paint.
And now in Church they speak in awe of Abraham and Moses;
Ezekiel's Wheel, and Joseph's Coat – and Cedric Rose's noses.

THE HAGGIS

Wi' a haggis in your sporran
And a caber up your kilt
And a pocket full of porridge on the hob,
You'll be roamin' in the gloamin'
Huntin' Haggis in the Glen,
Sayin' things like "Aye the noo" and "Hud yer gob."

Now the English and the Scots
Have never really hit it off –
Sworn enemies! But, when all's said and done,
When it's Rabbie Burns's birthday
And the whiskey's flowin' free
We can all still get together and have fun !

HAPPINESS

Happiness is like a bird which sings on yonder tree,
And if we look towards it, it flies away so free.
But if we look away from it; gaze this way and that,
The bird will fly towards us – and crap upon our hat.

We all want to get on well in our careers become successful and rise to the top...
or do we?

THE EXECUTIVE

He gets up in the morning, shaves his chin and combs his hair,
Then he travels to the office and he sits down in his chair.
His secretary's waiting with her pencil in her hand.
"Good morning, Brenda," he remarks, "now what have we got planned?"

"At ten o'clock sir," she replies, "you're meeting Mr Cross,
And at 11.30 there's a meeting with the Boss,
And then you've got a business lunch from 1 till half-past 2
And after that you must ring Mr Grimm, he's chasing you.

"Tomorrow, there's a conference in Leeds – I've booked your flight –
There won't be time for lunch because your schedule's very tight.
Oh, by the way, your Wife just rang – she's pressing for divorce –
I said you'd ring her back on Thursday – if you're free of course.

"On Friday, there's a meeting at the London Branch at three,
The Managing Director says it's top priority.
Next week your new assistant starts – that nice young Mr Spiers.
The Boss says he's a bright young chap with lots of new ideas.

"In April there's a takeover, in May they're cutting back.
I hear old Mr Hargreaves in Accounts will get the sack.
And next year you'll be transferred up to Liverpool from here.
In two years' time your duodenal ulcer will appear.

"Your nervous breakdown follows and the Boss says that it's best
If you take a few weeks off and have a long awaited rest.
You come back three weeks later feeling quite as good as new
And find your new assistant's been promoted over you.

"At sixty you'll have high-blood pressure and an aching back.
At sixty-two at work one day, you'll have a heart attack.
And while you're in the hospital the Boss will send a letter:
'We're pensioning you off Old Man – we hope you're feeling better.

"'We're sure you'll like retirement – no more stress or hurly-burly –
We can't give you a gold watch, 'cos we pensioned you off early.'
At least you'll get the pension – which is worth its weight in gold –
Though, of course you'll never spend it 'cos you'll be too bloody old.

"Of course, I'm just a secretary – that's all I'm fit to do sir,
I'll never be a really top executive, like you sir."

We all dream of becoming rich one day. This fellow did just that...
By the way, for those of you who don't remember, the 'Pools" (or 'Football Pools')
was what we used to do before the advent of the National Lottery.

EIGHT DRAWS UP

I used to be a tool setter, I'd work from eight to four,
And sometimes there'd be overtime to earn a few quid more,
And sometimes, when I'd finished work, I'd lay aside my tools,
And sit and dream how nice 'twould be if I could win the pools.

I used to read of winners, who said "money won't change me!
"I'll stay on at my prefab, working at the factory."
"Like hell!" I said. "If I was rich, I'd never work again,
I'd live a life of luxury and stay in bed 'till ten!"

We filled our coupon every week – that's me and my mate, Sid.
And then, one day, it happened: and we won two million quid!
My mates said "Blimey! Well done, lads – you sure know how to pick 'em."
I sorted out me tools and told the foreman where to stick 'em.

I bought me Mum a nice new house, and me Dad a Rolls Royce car,
And I took me mates to celebrate, down at Rosie's Bar.
Then Sid and me, we took advice and bought some stocks and shares.
We both learned fast and pretty soon were multi-millionaires.

I have an office and some staff – my empire's growing fast.
It's what I've always wanted – I've achieved my dream, at last.
I've got a house in Surrey and three chauffeur-driven cars.
It's caviar and 'champers' now, and great big fat cigars.

Of course, it isn't easy – my schedule's pretty tight.
I work from early morning until ten o'clock at night.
And sometimes, when I've finished work, I get out my old tools,
And sit and dream how nice it was before I won the pools.

THE RAIN

The rain it falleth on the rich
And on the poor as well, see?
It falleth on the Aga Khan
And on my Auntie Elsie.

Like poor old Oliver Court (see above) I'm on the short side.
Some people, however, have just the opposite problem...

JONATHAN WISE

Now Jonathan Wise was a hell of a size,
In fact he was six foot ten.
When he was seven he was five foot eleven,
And he'd never looked back since then.

He said to his wife "it's the bane of my life,
Being taller than most other people.
I can never play games, and my friends call me names
Like bean-pole or short-arse or steeple."

Said his wife, "Never fear, you mustn't fret dear,
Being tall is a blessing from heaven.
Walk tall and be proud with your head in a cloud,
And try to be six foot eleven."

So he stopped being shy, and he held his head high,
And he walked down the yard full of pride.
He went into his shed, and he just caught his head,
And he fractured his skull, and he died.

My wife and I still miss our collie, Caryad, who died a few years ago.
She was born in a farmyard barn (Caryad, that is, not my wife)
but came to live with us in Suburbia when she was still a puppy.

CARYAD

Caryad sleeps on a blanket warm,
Her nose between her paws.
Upstairs, the Mistress quietly sleeps,
The Master gently snores.

The carriage clock ticks on the mantelpiece,
The glowing embers die
And in the darkened street outside
A late-night car drones by.

But Caryad sleeps on her blanket warm,
Her nose between her paws,
And she dreams of the wind sweeping down from the hills
And rattling the old barn doors.

HENRY STILE

Henry Stile, by trade a vet,
Ate a 'phone book for a bet.
But a problem then he faced:
He found that he'd acquired a taste
For printed works. He gave up meat;
The written word was all he'd eat.
As befits a veterinarian,
He'd become a vegetarian.

His day began at half-past eight,
With the morning papers – on a plate.
At coffee break he liked a snack:
A page from *Old Moore's Almanac.*
When lunchtime came, he often took
A chapter from his library book,
Followed by *A Winter's Tale,*
Or extracts from the mid-day mail.

His literary taste, you see,
Was not confined, like you and me,
To books which we can read and savour;
He was more concerned with flavour.
"Artistic merit? Bosh!" he cried.
"I prefer 'em lightly fried.
A nice short story, slowly eaten,
In my opinion can't be beaten."

His friends advised that he should fight
This literary appetite.
One day they led him by the hand
To a restaurant in the Strand.
On reaching this exclusive venue;
He straight away devoured the menu.
His friends abandoned him at that.
He wrung his hands, and ate his hat.

He went along to Doctor Scrabbit
To ask for help to kick the habit.
The Doctor wrote him out a slip
To take to chemist, Mr Thripp.
He hurried out – no time to waste,
But on the way, you see, his taste
For printed works of all description
Made him eat his own prescription.

One morning, as he idly gnawed
A letter from his Auntie Maud,
A good idea to him came –
He could achieve both wealth and fame
By smashing world records galore
For eating literature – raw!
He thought he'd shovel down his throat
An Encyclopaedia of note.

But this is where the trouble starts –
It came in twenty-seven parts!
The attempt was filmed on BBC.
He started off with A and B
And munched his way right through to Z
And then, the index, bound in red.
"Bravo! Bravo!" the people cried.
Then Henry Stile lay down and died.

The British Public sadly mourned
Poor Henry Stile, who was once was scorn'd.
He'd given them a little fun;
Amidst the gloom, a ray of sun.
They buried him in pomp and state
In memory of what he ate.
The epitaph reads "Henry Stile –
A most distinguished bibliophile."

REBELLION

I hate my Mum; I hate my Dad; I hate my Auntie Flo!
I'd run away from home, if I could find somewhere to go.
It really isn't fair you know – I mean I'm only ten!
I've half a mind to go downstairs and stamp and shout again!

I hate it most of all when Auntie Flo comes here to tea.
They sit around and talk and talk – they never play with me.
Sometimes Auntie pats my head and says "how's little Billy?"
And when I say I'm feeling bored, they say I'm being silly!

I thought my Auntie Flo would like to see my new toy rifle –
Did they think it was on purpose that I dropped it in the trifle?
And then, when Mom got mad because I left my bread and butter,
Dad said I was cheeking her because he heard me mutter!

I really only thought it, so I don't know how he heard,
But he said that I must never ever use that dreadful word!
And then he sent me to my room, and that's why I'm up here,
Well, I know what I'll do – I'll make them sorry, never fear!

I'll stay up here for ever, in my bedroom, on my own,
I'll never eat nor drink again; I'll sit here all alone.
And soon I will be weak and ill – eventually, I'll die!
My Mom and Dad will mourn for me and Auntie Flo will cry.

And then perhaps they'll realise – but who's that on the stair?
It sounds a bit like Dad. But let him come up – I don't care!
..."Hello, Dad. Yes, I'm sorry – what must Auntie think of me?
D'you think I might come down now, and finish off my tea...?"

28

ROBERT MULDANE

Now Robert Muldane had a brilliant brain,
Any problem our Robert could figure.
But, in spite of this, Bob hadn't much of a job;
He drove a mechanical digger.

One day, Tessa, his wife, said "you're wasting your life,
I can't understand it," said Tessa.
"You use all your brains for the digging of drains,
When you could be a college professor."

Bob said, "I concede, I would doubtless succeed
As a Doctor of Medicine or Law,
But here I'll remain, for I firmly maintain
That I'm earning a bloody sight more!"

THE BUSKER

The Busker stands and plays his tunes beside the theatre queue.
The rain is slowly soaking through the hole in his left shoe.
Most people glance at him with scorn then look the other way.
Fourteen pence is all he's earned from standing here all day.

But he remembers better times, although he may not show it.
He was a man of substance once – a very famous poet.
A magazine commissioned him (a thousand pounds a go!)
To write an epic poem on the Chelsea Flower Show.

He thought it would be easy, shouldn't take more than an hour,
But oh, the shame, he failed the task because of one damn flower.
He's now reduced to begging pennies, playing his euphonium
And all because he couldn't find a rhyme for pelargonium.

ALEXANDER JAMES DUNBAR

Alexander James Dunbar
Bought himself a bubble car.
But he found, when testing it,
That his bagpipes would not fit
Inside the boot. Ah, cruel fate!
He took it back to remonstrate
And said that house-room he'd not give
To a vehicle so diminutive.

The salesman said: "Ah! Well, you see,
The Manufacturer's guarantee
Does not include a bagpipe clause –
You'll have to modify the doors.
You're all the same, you Scottish types –
You buy your cars to fit your pipes.
'Twould be more sensible by far
To make your bagpipes fit your car."

So Alexander went and bought a
Set of pipes six inches shorter.
Less expensive this, by far,
Than purchasing a bigger car.
He drove on home then, satisfied,
To take his missus for a ride –
But fate a further trick had played!
He's now attempting to persuade
A surgeon friend of his in Fife
To lop six inches off his wife.

PENELOPE POTTER

Penelope Potter was fond of her food,
And sometimes her friends would consider her rude;
When faced with a steaming hot pudding or pie
She'd scoff down the lot without batting an eye.
Pastries or pancakes, soups cold or hot,
Dumplings or doughnuts – she didn't mind what.
She wasn't concerned with the flavour as such;
The thing that most mattered to her was HOW MUCH!

One day as her meal was about to begin
(She'd picked up her fork and was getting stuck in)
A friend came to visit – a lady called Mabel
Who threw up her hands at the sight of the table.
She said "Oh Penelope, throw out that plate!
You must go on a diet like me and lose weight.
The rest of your meal you must put in the bin
To be thin is a virtue – being fat is a sin!"

A heated debate on the issues took place,
With each of them trying to argue her case;
Mabel insisting that dieting is good,
Penelope favouring chocolate pud.
They argued the point till they'd both had enough
And Mabel eventually left in a huff.

Now each thinks the other's an absolute rotter.
I personally side with Penelope Potter.

I don't mind a bit of DIY, in fact, I quite enjoy it – except when my efforts are viewed by an "expert." And if that "Expert" were my next door neighbour...

DIY DEREK

I've never been much of a practical chap –
I don't know a plane from a drill;
So if something goes wrong, like a leak in a tap,
I don't tear my hair out or get in a flap,
I call in a plumber to cure the mishap,
And ask him to send me the bill.

But the fellow next door, now he'll work without pause –
He'll tackle all jobs with no fear;
He's installed central heating and new garage doors,
He's laid down new floorboards on all of his floors,
He's fitted new wardrobes and made chests of drawers,
He even brews up his own beer.

Now, one day last April, my wife had a thought:
She said, "what we need is a shelf
To take those new leather-bound books that we've bought,"
So I suggested a joiner be sought,
But the fellow next door said, "why pay out, Old Sport?
You can easily do it yourself."

He lent me some wood and some screws and a saw
And said, "there you are, now have fun!"
So after I'd picked myself up from the floor,
I got down to work – and I worked my hands raw!
I hammered and drilled and I cursed and I swore
And after three weeks, it was done.

I must say, I felt justifiably proud,
As I called in my wife from the hall.
She said, "very nice!" and I graciously bowed.
Then, with a crash quite remarkably loud,
'Midst brick-dust and plaster which rose in a cloud,
The damn thing fell down from the wall!

As the cloud cleared and we opened our eyes
The extent of the damage we saw
Silent we stood, with a wild surmise,
She clutched at my hand and I felt my hair rise
It was, I admit, an unpleasant surprise –
We could both see right through to next door!

My neighbour was there – well, he got quite a fright.
I offered to pay right away
To bring in a builder that very same night.
He said "don't do that, why the damage is slight;
With some bricks and cement you can soon put it right.
It won't take you more than a day."

So I purchased the stuff, and it wasn't too dear,
And I laid out my tools on the table.
In a month it was done and I gave a loud cheer.
Then the lights all went out and I thought "now that's queer!"
In the course of my brick-laying efforts, I fear,
I'd pierced an electrical cable!

My neighbour said: "Ah! now I know just what's wrong:
Your house needs rewiring, that's all.
I did mine last year and it didn't take long;
You can purchase the cable and wire for a song.
Just make sure the wires go where they belong
And then channel them into the wall."

I called in my wife after three months of hell.
"It's done, dear," I nervously coughed.
I threw the main switch – had I done my job well?
Now was the time, only now could we tell.
My dear wife said, "what's that peculiar smell?"
I'd started a fire in the loft!

The fire quickly spread – soon the house was ablaze –
A sight I shall always remember.
We called 999 and walked round in a daze
As firemen fought bravely through smoke and through haze
But the house just burnt down right before our dull gaze
Right down to the last smoking ember.

Now we live in a tent – but you won't hear us moan!
And I keep my hand in with hard labour.
I've taken up stone-carving all on my own.
For weeks I've been working at night, all alone.
The result of my work is a statue of stone –
And beneath it…is my next-door neighbour.

THE LEARNED LAWYER

The learned lawyer, lean and lank,
Short of sight and long of shank,
Tries his best the judge to please,
With needle wit and practised ease;
But if, perchance, his case should fail,
And his client is sent to gaol,
Will he worry? No, not he!
He'll close his file and take his fee.

The dismal doctor, dark and dour,
Will treat them all, both rich and poor,
From private ulcers with great wealth,
To bunions on the National Health.
He'll do his best – he's very fair,
But if, despite his every care,
A patient should, alas, succumb –
There's plenty more where he came from.

The precious parson, pious and pink,
Through his spectacles will blink
As, from the pulpit each Lord's Day,
He shows his little flock the way.
And on those rare occasions when
A dissident arrives – why, then
He guides him and directs his feet –
To the Baptists down the street.

The serving soldier, stern and straight,
Will fight to keep Great Britain great.
Prowess in peacetime he'll display,
Until he's on a general's pay;
And when war comes his men will go
To join the charge to fight the foe.
He'll mourn the officers who led it –
While he stayed home to take the credit.

Doctors, lawyers, soldiers too,
Parsons – all professionals true.
We pay them tribute and fat fees –
But lesser mortals – what of these?
The lawyer's clerk, the vicar's wife,
The private who lays down his life,
The nurse who toils to make us well –
Are they noticed – are they hell!

But just imagine if you can,
An ordinary working man,
And offer him an office, grand,
With secretaries on every hand,
A big cigar and gold-rimmed glasses –
The key to the professional classes –
Would he take it if he could?
You bet your bloody life, he would!

Childhood – the time in our lives when we become who we are. I remember my
childhood with a good deal of pleasure. Some children, however, are less fortunate...

BILLY

Down among the foxgloves by the tennis court,
Billy makes a cardboard box into an island fort.
The soldiers are all ladybirds with tunics black and red
And Billy is the General by whom the troops are led.
The enemy is garden ants, who in their thousands swarm.
They give no quarter as they surge to take the fort by storm.
But General Billy's troops are firm as at their posts they stand –
A hand-selected fighting force – the bravest in the land.
But General Billy pauses as the ants prepare to flee.
A voice is heard from far away – "Billy! time for tea!"

Soon, the fort's abandoned and the troops for mercy beg,
And General Billy sits up straight to eat his boiled egg.
Auntie Ethel pours the tea; Aunt Joan picks up her fork.
Not a word is spoken, for it's rude to eat and talk.
Once, Billy had been out to tea with Timothy from school.
Timmy's Mum was very kind; his Dad had played the fool.
But, afterwards, his Auntie Joan was cross when he came in.
She said he was too boisterous and jam was on his chin.
So Timmy never asks him now, and Auntie Joan is glad.
Auntie Ethel says that Tim's a common village lad.
She says that Billy's lucky to have such a lovely home,
With fine big rooms to sit in and a garden he can roam.

But down among the foxgloves is Billy's favourite place.
There, it doesn't matter if there's jam upon his face.
To other folks, the tennis court is derelict and bare –
The net hangs torn, 'twixt rusted posts – a weedy, concrete square.
But other folks don't know, you see, that when they're back indoors,
The tennis court becomes a sea, with foxgloves on the shores.
The cardboard box becomes a ship, to sail the ocean free;
To voyage far to unknown lands beyond the willow tree.

On weekdays, Billy goes to school – he's in Miss Barstow's class,
She says he must try harder if exams he is to pass.
He sits by Jason Pumphrey, whom he hates with all his heart,
'Cos Jason pinches Billy's specs and tears his books apart.
Jason Pumphrey has a gang who wait outside the gates
And sometimes follow Billy home, crying "Fatty Four-eyes Bates!"

But down among the foxgloves, by the tennis court,
It doesn't really matter that he's fat and rather short.
There's no-one there to laugh at him and call him silly names;
He doesn't have to work out sums or join in stupid games.
His faithful crew will sail his ship across the ocean wide;
His troops are there to cheer him, as they rally to his side.
What cares he if Miss Barstow, Aunt Ethel and Aunt Joan
Say "he's an unattractive child – and always on his own."
Billy knows they're not to blame, they wouldn't understand
About the big, wide world of concrete sea and foxglove sand.
He knows he'll stay for ever with his soldiers in his fort,
Down among the foxgloves by the tennis court.

DRAGONS

I dreamed of dragons late last night
And woke to find my room was light;
Not sunshine bright as in the day,
But gently gleaming where I lay.

To my window then I crept,
While the household quietly slept.
I softly drew the curtains wide
And stood up tall to peek outside.

A vision in a window frame!
Familiar – yet not the same.
The lawn spread smoothly down below
All shimmering in a glimm'ring glow.

Beneath the oak tree's friendly shade,
Silvery shadows ran and played;
The holly bush stood, sparkly, stark,
Prickly glittering, light and dark.

This homely plot I know so well,
Now captured in this magic spell.
This special change in all I see;
What can this mean, how can this be?

And in my questing, wondering why?
I raise my eyes up to the sky
Where rides the moon, its friendly face
Smiling down through boundless space.

Why, there's the answer – Man's Old Friend,
Whose silken rays our troubles mend.
His kindly presence fills my head.
Monsters banished – back to bed!

AUTUMN

Sound the fanfare, raise your glasses,
Pass the plate for harvest home.
October's here and Summer passes,
Autumn calls us out to roam.

Sweeping leaves from paths and poking
Fallen twigs in plastic sacks;
Burning bonfires, softly smoking,
Tractors leaving big tyre tracks.

Tackling prickly bramble hedges,
Scratchy, thorny, fingers bleed;
Blackberries on meadow edges;
Bear them homeward with all speed.

Munching apples, crisply crunching,
Sipping cider, smoothly sweet.
Blustery winds to keep you hunching;
Dewy grass beneath your feet.

Fields and hedgerows each new morning
By the sun are gently kissed.
Wakening to greet the dawning,
Softened by the drifting mist.

SONNET

Of all the boons bestowed on Human kind
There is no finer blessing from above;
No matter how we search we shall not find
A gift more perfect or a greater love.
No other human virtue can compare,
In patience and in tolerant devotion,
To that unfettered, all-embracing care;
A deep affection – deeper than the ocean,
A love so freely given with such grace,
A tenderness which stands 'gainst all resistance,
A goodness which sustains the human race.
What is this prop, this staff of our existence?
The selfless gift of love so sweet and mild
Imparted by a Mother to her child.

We're all on a journey through life and none of us know for sure where we're going.
But at least we all know where we've been...

PERSPECTIVE

In the morning of our life the sun's before us;
Blinded by its light, we feel our way.
Who knows the mysteries that life holds for us;
Surprise and wonder greet us every day.

In the middle of our life, the sun is higher
And by its light, our path ahead is clear.
The present burns the past in all its fire
And we can face the future with no fear.

But things that happened to us in the past
Will reappear to seek us out and find us.
Because, in time, events their shadows cast,
...But only when the sun is low behind us.

DIVERSITY

The difference between we two
Is that I'm me and you are you.
Apart from that we're just the same –
Two players in the same old game.

Except perhaps that you are tall
And, as you see, I'm rather small.
Oh yes, of course, and you're a she
And, obviously, I'm a he.

But that aside, one cannot see
The slightest small disparity
Between we two – we could be one;
No differences to dwell upon.

Although your skin is clearly white
Whereas my own is black as night.
And there are different things we like –
You like to walk, I ride my bike.

I like rock music, you like swing;
I like Autumn, you like Spring.
And strangely – most importantly,
I like you and you like me.

'YOU'

Whilst boiling up a nice hot brew
And looking out some cake to chew,
I thought I'd give a thought or two
To rhyming verses – just a few,
But soon the poem grew and grew
Until the rhymes formed quite a queue
And pretty soon the time just flew.
I really should have stopped, it's true -
I had so many jobs to do,
Like mending that hole in my shoe
Or fixing broken chairs with glue;
Peeling onions for stew
Or painting kitchen cupboards blue,
(Or maybe some more subtle hue),
But minutes passed and hours too -
Where that time went, I never knew.
What happens now, I have no clue;
Can't find another rhyme...can you?

'AND?'

Come Rhymesters all throughout the land,
Rise up, rise up and make a stand;
Come beat the drum, strike up the band.
With fervour let the flames be fanned,
Let all the barricades be manned.
Forget those rhyming couplets bland
And all 'blank verses' must be banned.
Each one of us should turn our hand
To poems of a different brand –
An art which centuries has spanned:
Poetry where rhymes are planned
As numerous as grains of sand
No matter if our work is panned
By pompous critics, tall and tanned,
Let's activate our 'rhyming gland'
And make an everlasting strand
Of rhyming lines sublimely grand.
So now to you – the next line...and...?

SETTING UP

Moving house was much easier, ages ago:
You just found a nice cave to move in-ter.
With a handful of pins and some animal skins
You could keep yourself for warm for the Winter.

But now it's much harder than ever it was -
There are so many things to remember.
There's no time to shirk, there's quite enough work
From New Year right through to December.

There's walls to paper and all of that caper
And carpet to cover the floor with;
There's telephone bills and aspirin pills
And handles to open the door with.

There's electric and water and rooms that are shorter
Than beds which you bought to go in 'em;
There's fridges and freezers and hot water geysers
And things that you don't need – so bin 'em!

There's kettles and pans and extractor fans
And things that reduce you to boredom,
And hot-water tanks and letters from Banks
Which tell you, you just can't afford 'em.

There's choices of colour and things even duller
Like coathooks and sizes of curtain.
It's a question of taste – Oh, and wallpaper paste
And you'll need a good toolkit – that's certain.

These are just a few things (I forgot curtain rings!)
Which we all have to keep in our mind.
Setting up seems no fun – but when all the work's done
It's worth every minute you'll find!

HAMMOND HALL

'Twas Sunday, the family had just finished lunch,
And Mother and Father said, "Listen you bunch,
We'd like an hour's peace, so be good and no noise,
Go and play quietly, like good little boys."
So Richard and Andrew and Nicholas too,
Went out in the garden saying, "What shall we do?"
Richard said, "I know, lets do something good,
To help Mum and Dad, 'cos I think that we should."
Andrew said, "I know a good thing to do,
We could decorate their bedroom,"
And Nick said, "Me too!"

So they went in the garage with no time to waste,
And got all the paint, and the paper and paste,
Then they all trooped upstairs just as quiet as they could
So as not to wake Daddy – now wasn't that good?
Said Richard, "The ceiling's the first thing to do,
I'd better do that 'cos I'm taller than you."
"OK, then," said Andy, "I'm going for a wee,
Then I'll do the door-frame,"
And Nick said, "And me."

So they all got to work, Richard stood on a chair
And painted the ceiling and most of his hair.
Andrew soon started off at a furious pace,
Splashing paint on the door-frame, his arms and his face.
Said Richard, "It's hard work, my arm's killing me,
I think we should rest now" – and Nick said, "And me."
"I'll get down off the chair for a bit," Richard said,
But he slipped and fell right onto Mom and Dad's bed
His paint pot went flying and landed on Nick,
Who swallowed a lot of the paint and was sick
All over Andy, who said, "Goodness me –
Dad's going to kill us," and Nick said, "And me."

48

Well they stood and they looked at the mess on the floor
And the mess on the walls and the bed and the door
Then they ran down the stairs for a bucket and mop
And they worked and they worked till they thought they would drop
Until every last bit was as clean as could be
And Rich said, "Thank goodness," and Nick said, "And me."
Then Mummy and Daddy came upstairs to see
And what a surprise they got: "Good gracious me!"
Mummy said, "well, what a nice thing to do,
They must have worked hard, I think, Daddy, don't you?"
Richard and Andrew said, "Easy peasy,"
And Daddy said, "Well done," and Nick said – "And me!"

THE ALMOST MAN

As a child, he was clever and popular
– Always played the fool
He almost gained a scholarship
To a well known public school.

Instead, he attended a secondary mod
In his home town of Berkhamstead
And was almost selected to join the A stream
But entered the B stream instead.

He'd fallen in love as a young man –
For ever, or so he thought;
She meant almost everything to him
But sadly it came to nought.

He almost joined the Navy then,
Prepared for a life at sea;
But, at the last moment, decided to switch
To a job in Accountancy.

Determined to make a go of it,
To a London firm he applied.
He almost attended an interview
But put the idea aside.

He accepted a post at Sainsbury's,
Stacking shelves and manning the tills.
Earning almost enough to pay the rent
As well as the grocery bills.

Arriving at work one morning,
He suffered a serious stroke.
"I almost think I'm dying"
Were the very last words he spoke.

He survived but was deep in a coma.
His friends and his family grieved.
Some people say that he almost died
But, really, he almost lived.

A CUB SCOUT'S PROMISE

The other cubs are playing clarinets and all that stuff.
But Akela says I can't be in the show – I'm much too rough.
I don't think I'm rough at all – I'm really very clever;
I'm never naughty, never bad at all – well, hardly ever!

I know I shot the Group Scout Leader with my catapult –
But the frog in Carla's handbag – well, it just was not my fault!
Just because when we went camping, I fell in the river,
The Leaders say the sight of me just makes them sort of... shiver.

Akela says my uniform's an absolute disgrace,
Just because my socks are down and jam is on my face.
He says my woggle's wonky and my cap is never straight,
But what does he expect – the Coldstream Guards? I'm only eight.

My brother is a sixer, he's got badges everywhere;
His neckerchief is spotless and he always combs his hair.
Akela says he's proud of him, he's all a cub should be –
He says I should be more like him and not so much like me.

But, one day soon, perhaps I'll be a sixer like my brother –
I'll pull my socks up then and be as smart as any other.
I'll straighten up my neckerchief and cap like all the rest –
Akela will be proud of ME – 'cos I'll have done my best!

ST GEORGE AND THE DRAGON

They asked…who killed the dragon?
Whoever could it be?
Who bravely slew the evil beast
And set Old England free?
Such gallantry should be acclaimed
For all the World to see!
They asked…who killed the dragon?
George whispered:……"it was me…"

What's your idea of a "Club"? A tennis club, a knitting club, a Pall Mall establishment, a book club, a night club? Everyone has their own idea of what "A Club" is – so the misunderstanding in this case was surely forgiveable...

GONE CLUBBING

My friend said: "this evening I'm off to a Club,"
But I said I'd much rather go down the pub.
My friend said ,"Why's that? You don't sound very keen."
I said, "I don't go clubbing – just not my scene.
I don't much like music so loud you can't think,
I really prefer just to have a quiet drink.
And what turns me on is not heroin or coke,
But chatting to people and mixing with folk."

"Ah, well," said my friend, "if that's really your thing,
Come along there tonight – it'll sure make you sing!"
"I doubt it," I thought but I must be polite,
So I said: "well, I'll come. I won't put up a fight."
He came round in his car at a quarter to eight.
I got in with a groan and submitted to fate.
He turned left at the crossroads, which caused me to frown.
The nightclubs were all in the centre of town.

He drove down some lanes with a satisfied sigh
And pulled up at a pub in a village nearby.
I said "now just hang on, this doesn't seem right.
I thought we were going to go clubbing tonight."
"That's just what we're doing," he said and got out.
I followed him, wondering what this was about.
We went into the pub and he bought me a beer,
Then we climbed up some stairs and were met with a cheer!

Lots of people were there, supping ale with a smile.
I was glad to join with them – and, after a while,
Some fellow got up and he sang us a song.
When it came to the chorus, we all sang along!
Then others stood up, one by one, just to sing
Causing spirits to soar and the rafters to ring.
Songs of the countryside, songs of the sea;
Songs about people just like you and me.

Some songs were old – straight from history's pages;
Songs which have stayed with us all through the ages.
Songs from the past from which all of us came.
Now life is so different, yet we're still the same.
After that evening, I'm left in no doubt
That friendship and sharing are what it's about.
Now I'm learning a song – that's how I'm spending my day
And I'm off to the Folk Club to sing it next Friday.

A TRIBUTE TO WESTON

Where is this place which lies serene, beneath a flawless sky?
'Tis Weston-under-Penyard, near the town of Ross-on-Wye.
With green fields all around it, so peaceful and so still,
The village nestles, tranquil, in the shade of Penyard Hill.
The Weston Cross sits, cosily, a meeting place for all,
And for those special prime events – the bustling Village Hall.
The Church stands high – for centuries a sanctuary of peace,
A haven there for everyone – and may it never cease.
The village school is full of life – a place of fun and laughter,
Where children learn those lessons they'll remember ever after.
Yes, there are times when skies are grey – when clouds obscure the light.
Times when the future seems unsure – when day turns into night.
But, through it all – the villagers, no matter what the weather.
It's they who make it all worth while – long may we work together.

INFINITE VARIETY

We are individuals, each one of us unique.
If ever it were otherwise, the future would be bleak.
Imagine if there came a time when we were all the same;
No differences between us – same looks, same sex, same name;
If we all shared the same opinions, likes, and dislikes too.
There'd be no need for anyone, nothing left to do.

Variety is infinite – that shouldn't cause us strife.
Each day we find new things to do, new ways to look at life.
I like to walk, you like to drive, I like meat, you like veg.,
I like my feet on solid ground, you live life on the edge.
I think the world of my pet dog, you may prefer your cat,
I rise at dawn, you get up late – there's nothing wrong with that.

Our differences should not just lead to weary toleration.
Those differences should give us cause for joyful celebration.
This world we were born into brings fresh challenges each day,
Sometimes life is hard to cope with, struggle as we may.
Sometimes it's light, sometimes it's dark – sometimes it's stormy weather.
But, when you come right down to it – *we're all in it together.*

THE OLD PHOTO

It's just a photograph, that's all;
A picture hanging on the wall.
I've walked straight past it every day
For more years than I like to say.
The glass is chipped, obscured by dust;
The metal frame adorned with rust.
The picture – once as bright as day,
Now is yellowed, dark and grey.
The face within, that hair, those eyes,
That kindly smile which never dies
Still uplifts me like no other –
She who gave me life – my Mother.

THE RUNAWAY

Life can be difficult, life can be cruel
But I'm out on the road with a full tank of fuel.
The hills in the distance, the sky over all;
I can just be myself, be proud and walk tall
I can go where I like and do what I choose,
I have nothing to fear, I have nothing to lose.

I don't know where I'm going, but when I get there,
I'll stand and I'll say to myself – "well, now where?
I'm here as a stranger – where should I go?
Look round at the people – there's no-one I know."
I'll lift up my eyes to the heavens above.
Then I'll drive home to the ones that I love.

Don't get me wrong – Ambition's a fine thing. But we do have to be realistic...

DISILLUSIONMENT

When I was a boy I was told to try hard
To better myself and aim high
"There's no limit," they said, "to what you can achieve,
So reach for the stars in the sky."

They said I could go to wherever I pleased
Be whatever I wanted to be.
I believed them and thought I could rise to great heights –
Banish all doubts and be free!

But now I've grown up and achieved common sense,
I don't reach for the stars any more.
The stars are millions of miles above –
And I'm only five foot four!

HUMAN KNOWLEDGE

What a wondrous thing is the Human Race –
A species of infinite worth.
Our planet began as a lifeless sphere –
The planet we now know as Earth.

We developed ourselves from primitive apes
To masters of all we survey.
We now understand how the universe works;
We know how the night follows day.

We know how our planet encircles the Sun;
We're able to travel through space;
We know about gravity, atmosphere, life;
We know how the stars stay in place.

Evolution is something we now understand;
How species develop and grow
From primitive creatures to beings like us –
That's something we've now come to know.

Our knowledge increased over thousands of years.
We've grown from the earth to the sky.
We now understand how it all came about.
The thing that we don't know is...WHY?

We all have to deal as best we can with whatever life throws at us as. Of course,
some have more thrown at them than others...

HOME TERRITORY

When I was ten I'd play hide and seek
With my mates and, just for a lark,
I'd run to my favourite hiding place –
Under a hedge in the park.

Then, when I was fifteen, my parents both died
In a car crash – such things do occur.
My aunt took me in – there was nobody else,
So I stayed in her house for a year.

Then I left school and met up with some guys
Who introduced me to cocaine.
My aunt kicked me out so I wandered around
And looked for a job – but in vain.

I met up with a mate who took pity on me
So I slept on the floor in his flat.
But he ran out of money for paying his rent
So that put an ending to that.

I begged on the streets for a couple of years,
For pennies – that's all I could get
I slept on a bench in the square every night,
But that's no damn good when it's wet.

So now I've moved on and I've found what to do:
Whenever it rains and gets dark
I just run back here to my favourite place –
Under a hedge in the park.